HOPE
In The Ruins

A Rescue and Recovery Plan for Hearts in Crisis

LORI BORUFF

ISBN 978-0-615-93521-8
ISBN 13: 9780615935218

DEDICATED TO

My Living Hope, Jesus Christ, who gave his life for mine; my husband, Rick, and family who shares their life with mine; my mother, Cherie and my friends, who dream big dreams and believed in mine.

Table of Contents

INTRODUCTION

The Power of Hope

Natural disasters like floods, fires, tornadoes, hurricanes and earthquakes unexpectedly strike creating chaos and hopelessness.

Top it off with man-made disasters like disease, shootings, kidnappings, and terrorist attacks. Soon, all hope is gone.

These natural and man-made catastrophes require a rescue, recovery and rebuilding plan. Within minutes, first responders are to the rescue. Hours and sometimes days are spent with hopes of recovering the wounded and lost.

Entire nations celebrate when someone emerges alive from the ruins. Hope comes alive! With hard work, perseverance and courage—the rebuilding begins.

Following September 11, 2001 after 3000 innocent people perished in a series of terrorist attacks, all hope seemed lost.

In New York City where once The World Trade Towers stood tall as a symbol of peace, Mayor Rudy Giuliani proclaimed, "We will rebuild. We're going to come out of this stronger than before..." And, they did. Hope was restored to Ground Zero.

You also have hope in the ruins.

As you look at the destruction in your life caused by a natural or man-made disaster, you may be paralyzed by fear. You may be overwhelmed. You may be asking, "Where is hope?"

I know the feeling!

When I discovered the right tools to help me dig through the rubble of fear, unforgiveness, and disappointment—I found hope again.

All the tools are in this little book. Keep moving forward and you too, will rebuild your life stronger than before.

Hope isn't optional. It's essential to our survival... Hope is basic to life. Take away our hope, and our existence is reduced to depression and despair.
-Author Charles R. Swindoll, The Rising Hope

WHERE IS HOPE?

Where is hope when man-made disasters strike the heart? Adultery, divorce, abuse, rape, financial collapse destroys lives. The ripple effect devastates generations.

Have tons of debris like fear, unforgiveness, rejection, abandonment, betrayal and resentment covered your heart and left you feeling hopeless? Is it hard to breathe and you sense anxiety and panic? Do you have the answer to the question *Where is hope?*

I FOUND HOPE BURIED IN THE RUINS.

My world crashed when an arresting officer handcuffed our teenage son and drove away—down the road of uncertainty. Rusty was charged with two Class X felonies and being held on $200,000 bond.

As the debris of disappointment and fragments of fear settled over my broken heart—I could not find any hope.

This was not on my radar screen.

Fear paralyzed me.
Hopelessness suffocated me.
Now what?

How do I help my son when I felt helpless? How do I encourage my son when I felt hopeless?

It was time to implement a rescue and recovery plan and rebuild my life stronger than before.

> *I know the power of hope because I have experience it.*
> - Lori Boruff

RESCUE

In the midst of my pain, I cried out to my rescuer—Jesus Christ, my first responder.

Since I have you, Jesus, I have hope—but where is it?
He whispered to my heart...
It's buried in the ruins.

That heavenly thought reminded me it's impossible to lose hope when Jesus Christ is my Living Hope. I simply need to dig through the rubble to find hope again.

RECOVERY

As I picked up each piece of emotional pain and hauled it to Jesus through prayer—I began the recovery process. Hope quickly restored my broken heart. Living Hope gave me the perspective and power I needed to get out of bed every day.

Living Hope helped me love my son unconditionally.
Living Hope held my hand in the courtroom.

Living Hope took me to jail early on visiting days and kept me late. I reached out to hurting families experiencing their own personal 9/11's.

I needed Living Hope because without it, nothing made sense.

REBUILD

After tons of fear, unforgiveness and disappointment were hauled away—I could rebuild. God transformed that mess into a message which I share with thousands of hearts in crisis.

Rusty also experienced Living Hope! In cell 121 at his darkest moment, Jesus became real to him. He found hope in the ruins. His life quickly rebuilt into a life-changing ministry called One Eighty. You, too, can experience the power of HOPE!

~ **1** ~

THE FIRST RESPONDER

There is surely a future hope for you,
And your hope will not be cut off.
Proverbs 23:18 NIV

Who is your first responder?
Why would he risk everything for you?

God sees a dying and hopeless world. Out of love, He sends his perfect son, Jesus Christ to rescue imperfect and hurting people. He freely offers Living Hope to anyone who wishes to experience never-ending freedom, joy, peace and hope.

For God so loved the world so much that he gave his one and only
Son, so that everyone who believes in him will not perish but
have eternal life. God sent his Son into the world not to judge the
world, but to save the world through him.
John3:16-17 NLT

Jesus gave his life for me—and for you. His death was cruel and undeserved yet, necessary for the benefit of all who desire Living Hope and the promise of heaven.

> **Christ lived the life we could not live**
> **and took the punishment we could not take**
> **to offer the hope we cannot resist.**
> -Max Lucado, *Hope Pure and Simple*

If you confess with your mouth that Jesus is Lord
and believe in your heart that God
raised him from the dead, you will be saved.
Romans 10:9 NLT

Do you have that Living Hope?

It's simple as 1, 2, 3! Just believe!

1) Believe that Jesus is God's son who came to earth as a perfect man and died on the cross for imperfect people like you and me.

2) Believe that three days later, He rose from the grave to live with God in heaven and is preparing a home for you.

3) Confess with your mouth that Jesus Christ is Lord.

To bring Living Hope into your heart, pray this simple prayer:

Jesus,

I need hope. I need you. I believe that you are God's only and perfect son that came to earth to save imperfect people like me.

I know I go against God. I've had my back turned to Him. But today, I simply say "I believe."

I believe that you, Jesus, died on the cross in my place. I believe you rose from the grave and that you are in heaven waiting for me. I believe that out of love, You are my first responder. You saved me.

Today, I want to love you back by saying "I believe." Jesus Christ, you are LORD!

In your name, Jesus, I believe!

You are saved and now have Hope in the Ruins!

Today's Date:

Write a personal prayer of thanks:

Dear Jesus,

Thank you,

Beloved, I wish above all things that you would prosper
and be in health, even as your soul prospers.
3 John 1:2 NKJV

On the hard days through the recovery process, your WHY will motivate you to keep moving forward. Which WHY resonates with you?

15 Reasons to Heal and Get Real

1. Gain inner confidence to take you to new levels in relationships, work and play.
2. Learn to *respond* to offenses rather than re-act to them.
3. Experience restored relationships.
4. Live in peace—even in the storms of life.
5. Give and receive love with greater ability.
6. Develop a deeper faith to take you to higher places.
7. Discover ways to positively affect others.
8. Take risks—love more, trust more, give more.
9. Receive a new perspective on people and your circumstances.
10. Break the generational cycle of hurting people hurting people.
11. Remember the past without re-living the pain.
12. Improve your physical health.
13. Uncover dead dreams and watch them come to life.
14. Operate out of abundance of hope which overflows to those around you.
15. Live in line with God's desire for you.

What are your top three reasons to heal and get real?
1)
2)
3)

~ 2 ~

THINK H.O.P.E. – EVERY DAY

As for me, I will always have hope...
Psalm 71:14 NIV

A Four-Step Formula for Healing and Health

Emotional pain keeps us from seeing life clearly. Trusting a hurting heart is like driving down a mountain through a thick morning fog. It can be dangerous.

My son's arrest created a foggy future. The fear of not knowing was paralyzing. Forgiveness seemed too dangerous. Disappointment snuck up on me and pushed me over the edge.

Thinking H.O.P.E. everyday clears up the fog. This simple step-by-step formula brings order to the healing process and deters overwhelmed feelings which can stop us in our tracks. It's like a GPS guiding us through those haunting questions—*Where do I start? Where am I going? How do I get there?*

Do you find your *Good Mornings* filled with negative thoughts and weighing you down? Do you start your day without a plan of action and soon feel you are drowning in hopelessness?

We all need a daily check up—from the neck up to avoid stinkin' thinkin'—which ultimately leads to hardening of the ATTITUDES.
Zig Ziglar, Motivational Speaker

H.O.P.E. every day goes beyond positive thinking! It changes your belief system.

What is the H.O.P.E. Formula?

STEP 1:

H is for HEALING:
- If you have a cold, you call a _____.
- If your car won't start, you call a _____.
- If you have a toothache, you call a _____.
- If you have a hurting heart, you call _____.

A doctor offers cold remedies; a mechanic repairs cars; a dentist soothes toothaches and JESUS heals hurting hearts.

So why don't people call on Jesus for healing broken and beaten hearts?

Why do people survive life rather that thrive in a life of hope?

Are you surviving or thriving? _____

Did you realize survival mode is costly?

Check which areas *living in survival* mode have cost you:

☐ Relationships are damaged or lost.

☐ Time is wasted when paralyzed by pain.

☐ Energy is drained and life is unproductive.

☐ Bank accounts are depleted through poor choices.

☐ Fun is sucked away.

☐ Joy and dreams are stolen.

☐ Physical health is infected by emotional pain.

What additional ways is emotional pain costIng you?

STEP 2:

O is for OVERCOMING:

Are you living as an overcomer based on your true identity through Jesus Christ, or just plain over-come with lies while surviving and living with a false identity?

It's important to understand your true identity as God's child. Those truths empower you to thrive!

God also tells us to take every thought captive (2 Corinthians 10:5). If you think that is impossible—you believe a lie.

God never sets us up to fail. He equips us with truth from His Word and with the mind of Christ. If God says to take every thought captive—you can do it!

**IF SATAN CAN CONTROL YOUR THOUGHTS,
HE CAN CONTROL YOUR LIFE.**

Who is controlling your thoughts? _____
Many medical professionals believe our thought life creates or adds to health issues like heart disease, cancer, depression and many more illnesses.

**EMOTIONAL PAIN FROM YOUR PAST
INFECTS YOUR FUTURE HEALTH AND HAPPINESS.**

What if the *cure* for physical healing was rooted in our emotional healing?

What if we could *prevent* physical diseases by learning how to process our emotional pain?

In the next chapter, I share the tools and insights which helped me live healthier and emotionally pain free! When you use those tools, you may find freedom too!

STEP 3:

P is for PURPOSE:

We are made by God—for God. Thanks to the very first couple created, and the fact that they believed a lie—we live in an imperfect world full of pain and tragedy. (Read Genesis 2 & 3)

**UNTIL WE FIND PURPOSE IN OUR PAIN,
LIFE WILL NOT MAKE SENSE.**

What in your past or present life is not making sense?

**GOD WANTS TO USE YOU BECAUSE OF YOUR PAIN,
NOT IN SPITE OF IT.**

Are you ready to discover purpose, direction, and dreams for your life and leave a lasting legacy?   YES   or   NO   (maybe isn't an option)

STEP 4:

E is for ENJOY:

It is impossible to overdose on JOY and HOPE!

A happy heart makes the face cheerful.
Proverbs 15:13 NIV

At first, you must be intentional about enjoying your changed life. As your heart heals, joy and hope will overflow and become contagious to those around you. It's fun to be free!

THINK H.O.P.E. EVERY DAY

These four steps are the formula you need to think H.O.P.E. every day. You will find balance between caring for your heart, thinking truth, finding purpose and enjoying a changed life. (A printable PDF is at www.LoriBoruff.com)

STEP 1 – HEAL

☐ Do I trust God with _____?

☐ Do I choose fear or hope in _____?

☐ I need to forgive _____.

☐ Today, I am putting my expectations in God regarding

_____.

STEP 2 – OVERCOME

☐ This is my true identity: _____.

☐ My first thought of the day: _____.

☐ Is it truth or a lie? The truth is

_____.

STEP 3 – PURPOSE

☐ How can God use me because of my pain, not in spite of it? _____.

☐ What is the dream God has put in my heart?

_____.

STEP 4 – ENJOY

• Today I will take a joy break and find joy in

_____.

Congrats! You completed your daily H.O.P.E. check-up from the neck-up!

~ **3** ~

LET THE HEALING BEGIN

The main step to healing is to acknowledge you are hurting.

Following my personal 9/11, my heart looked like debris piles. What does your heart in crisis look like?

| Draw a picture of your heart. | OR | What words describe your heart? |

Emotional pain is not pretty and we tend to look away—hoping it will go away! However, it doesn't. Often times it's destructive to our relationships, careers and life dreams.

IT TAKES LESS ENERGY AND EMOTIONAL EFFORT TO PROCESS THE PAIN THAN TO SPEND YEARS AVOIDING IT.

Think H.O.P.E.

STRIVE OR THRIVE?

> *May he be enthroned in God's presence forever; appoint your love and faithfulness to protect him.*
> Psalm 61:7 NIV

When life hurts, do you ignore the emotional pain? Do you coast on the road of life, detouring around the pain? Which excuse has become your comfort zone keeping you from thriving in life?

#1 Survival mode seems safer.

Really? How's that working for you? Emotional pain powerfully affects your perspective and decisions. Those clouded judgments turn what could be a spring rain into a thunderstorm. Are you experiencing stormy weather in your relationships, work and finances?

#2 I don't have the energy to process the pain.

Exactly! Emotional pain is a drain on energy, health, finance, joy, peace, love and LIFE! A good dose of hope can fix all that.

#3 I don't know how to process the pain.

Perfect! For such a time as this—today is the day to step into a changed life through education and integration. You will learn how you are wired and integrate your faith. The core principles throughout the four step formula give you a lifetime of tools to process the yuck keeping you stuck!

There are two basic psychological insights which were foundational in my healing process. I'll share those with you but please seek professional counseling if you sense a deeper need.

STEP 1:   HEAL

TWO TRANSFORMATIONAL TRUTHS
TO SET YOU FREE

TRUTH #1   COMPARTMENTALIZING PAIN

Our all-knowing and faithful God designed individuals with the ability to survive emotional pain by allowing us to compartmentalize fear, rejection, betrayal and much more.

THE PROBLEM IS WE DON'T REALIZE THAT TRUTH!

Christian are like smartphones complete with apps. Pinterest, Facebook, Gmail, Photos all have different functions making navigation easy to complete a specific task. Without apps, your smartphone would be a dumbphone because it would be impossible to find the function you need. It would be overwhelming.

Christians have different apps that function in different ways. The daughter or son app may operate with abuse. The wife app may hold betrayal. The little boy or girl app may function in fear. The 13 year old part of you app may not work properly because it doesn't feel good enough.

Once you recognize each part of you holds its own emotional pain, the healing process becomes more manageable. It's not so overwhelming!

God does not give us more that we can handle. This leads me to understand why our pain is compartmentalized and the benefits of that wisdom.

You may believe your faith is weak when in reality, another part needs healing. We have many layers or "apps" and it's a process to work through.

We function and feel as a child, teenage, man, woman, husband, wife, mother, father, grandparent, sister, brother, friend, co-worker and many more parts!

How many parts are inside the Christian part of you?

Write them here or use the diagram on page 23. A printable PDF is available at www.LoriBoruff.com/resources.

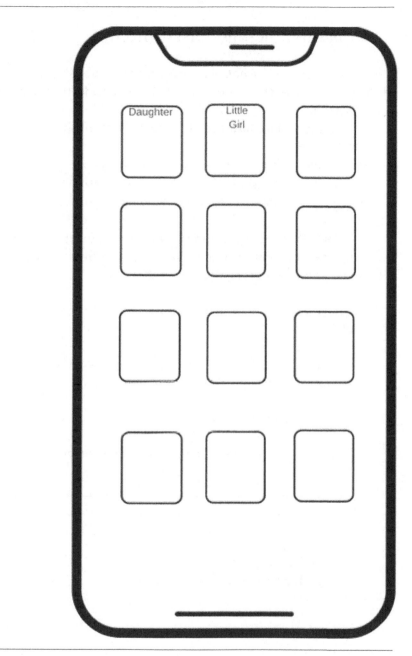

Daughter

Little
Girl

TRUTH #2   IDENTIFY FALSE PROTECTORS

The second psychological insight is false protectors. Hurting people use protectors to guard their heart from feeling emotional pain.

On the surface, protectors come in different shapes, sizes and forms like—

- People: spouse, parent, child or even pastor
- Food: sugar, candy, chocolate, caffeine, etc.
- Emotions: fake smile, anger, laughing

Have you turned to a spouse with the expectation he or she would say the right thing to make you feel better rather than turn to Jesus for comforting your wounds?

Have you ever indulged in comfort foods to deal with the stress of life?

Have you ever flashed a fake smile and a #Iamfine when inside your heart is aching and you want to cry?

We all use false protectors without a flinch of an eye.

Who or what do you turn towards when you are hurting?

_____

_____

_____

These false protectors are on the surface.
But, others live below the surface!

Let us dig a little deeper into a few psychological defenses like avoidance, rationalization, or denial that keeps us from processing our emotional pain in a healthy way.

Here are a few psychological defenses:

Avoidance: We know there is pain but we don't deal with it. Ex: *I'll deal with it later.*

Minimization: We reduce the size of the trauma. Ex: *many women are abused or my childhood wasn't that bad.*

Rationalization: We use rational arguments to justify behavior. Ex: *I was young or I deserved it.*

Denial: Refuse to acknowledge the truth. It feels safer than reality. Ex: *I never had sex with Monica Lewinsky!*

Perfectionism: It protects someone from their fear of rejection. Perfectionism has two extremes: *I can't do it right so I'm not going to try. OR, I want everything to be perfect and I'll drive everyone crazy in the process!*

Dissociation: A person dissociates from the situation or trauma. Mild case are daydreaming or getting lost in a moment. Severe cases result in multiple personalities.

HERE IS THE GOOD NEWS—
GOD ALLOWS PSYCHOLOGICAL DEFENSES TO MANAGE PAIN.

> *There are psychological defenses to help a child reduce the size of the trauma or stress so they can manage it with their child sized emotional resources.*
> - Dr. Karl Lehman

THANK GOD FOR THOSE PROTECTORS! BUT...
HERE COMES THE PROBLEM—

We don't get past this place. We get comfortable with those protectors rather than allowing God to be our Protector.

GOD, ALONE, WANTS TO BE OUR PROTECTOR!

In order to go deeper with God—he must be your protector. If he is nudging you to heal but you stay in your comfort zone trusting false protectors—that creates sin. Now, that creates a bigger problem!

When you become aware of this truth, it is necessary to break up with those false protectors and send them packing! Trust God completely to be your protector. He will never leave you.

Check which false protectors you need to break up with:

☐ Avoidance - *I'll deal with this later.*

☐ Minimization - *My pain really isn't so bad.*

☐ Rationalization - *I deserved what happened.*

☐ Denial – *I don't feel anything.*

☐ Perfectionism – *I'm not even going to try.*

☐ Dissociation - *I don't remember anything.*

Which parts of you need to pray the Protector Prayer on the next page?

_____ _____ _____
_____ _____ _____
_____ _____ _____

THE PROTECTOR PRAYER

Lord, the _____part of me is coming to you today. Thank you for the false protectors of _____(see below) to help me survive _____(trauma/stress).

But, now I want you to be my Protector. From this point forward trusting a false protector would be sin in my life. It hinders my healing and I miss your best for my life.

I confess and release using (defenses) _____ in my life.

Today, you alone are my Protector as I face _____(trauma/stress). I trust in your plan. I pray this by the power of your blood, power of your word and power of your name—Jesus Christ, my Living Hope. Amen.

Avoidance:	acknowledge but deal with it later
Minimization:	reduce size of sin/trauma/stress
Rationalization:	justifies behavior
Denial:	refuse to acknowledge truth
Perfectionism:	fear of rejection
Dissociation:	mind disconnects – no memory

TODAY, I DECLARE GOD IS MY PROTECTOR

Today's date:
Signature:

Refer to this prayer often as God reveals more layers to process. Remember, he does not give you more than you can handle.

PROMISES AND PRAYERS

God guards me:
Psalm 91:11 NIV – *for he will command his angels concerning you to guard you in all your ways.* **Thank you Lord, for commanding your angels to guard me in all my ways.**

Proverbs 2:11 NIV – *Discretion will protect you, and understanding will guard you.* **Thank you Lord, your discretion will protect me and your understanding will guard me.**

God preserves me:
Psalm 36:6 NIV – *Your righteousness is like the mighty mountains, your justice like the great deep. O Lord, you preserve both man and beast.* **Thank you Lord, your righteousness does not move, it is like a mighty mountain. Your justice is deeper than I can imagine. You, O Lord, preserve me.**

Psalm 41:2 NIV – *The LORD will protect him and preserve his life; he will bless him in the land and not surrender him to the desire of his foes.* **Thank you Lord, for protecting and preserving my life!**

God protects me:
Psalm 25:21 NIV – *May integrity and uprightness protect me, because my hope is in you.* **Thank you Lord, your integrity and uprightness protect me. They are my bodyguards because my hope is in you.**

Write your own promise and prayer here:

Who is it that overcomes the world? Only the one who believes
Jesus is the Son of God.
I John 5:3-5 NIV

STEP 2: OVERCOME

OVERCOME LIES WITH THRUTHS ABOUT YOUR TRUE IDENTITY SETS YOU FREE!

The moment you believe Jesus is the Son of God, you received a new identity. Once a sinner—now, a saint who sins.

Everything you need to rise above your circumstances is in you because Jesus is in you.

Does that perspective empower you to live like the overcomer you are? Stop striving to overcome. Ask Jesus to *release* what is already in you.

"Understanding your identity in Christ is absolutely essential for your success at living a victorious Christian life!"
- Dr. Neil T. Anderson, *Who I Am In Christ*
Gospel Light, 1993

So, why do we often feel defeated and just plain overcome? Because a part of us believes the lie we NEED to overcome when the truth is—we ARE overcomers.

This core principle from God's Word is life changing. Does it give you hope that you can be free from anger, depression, hopelessness and more?

What part of you needs to believe this truth?

The Identity Thief is alive and well. However, God's truth always prevails. Here are some more truths about your TRUE identity:

Satan's Lies	God's Truth
You are a sinner because you sin.	You are a saint who sins.
Your identity comes from what you have done.	Your identity comes from what God has done.
Your identity comes from what people say about you.	Your identity comes from what God says about you.
Your behavior tells you what to believe about yourself.	Your belief about yourself determines your behavior.

- From *My Identity,* Freedom In Christ Ministries

From this list of lies vs. truths, which one resonates with you?

Satan's lie: God's truth:

_____   _____

_____   _____

_____   _____

**The more you reaffirm who you are in Christ,
the more your behavior will begin to reflect
your true identity.
-Dr. Neil T. Anderson, Victory Over Darkness**

HOW DOES AN OVERCOMER PRAY?

Because we are overcomers, our prayers should be different. Pray like you already have the answer because you do! Try this—pray the answer not the problem!

Unlock the heavens with your belief!

Author of *Prayer Strategy,* Ruth Shinness-Brinduse, believes praying scripture gives you greater awareness of His Presence. "The more time I spent agreeing with Heaven, the more Heaven would be manifested in my earthly realm," writes Brinduse.

This is how I prayed before I understood Ruth's strategy:
Lord, I want to trust in you with all my heart. I'm trying to acknowledge you in all my ways but I need your help. Please help!
Today, this is my believing prayer taken from God's Word— Proverbs 3:5-6
Thank you LORD, that I trust in you with all my heart. I don't lean on my own understanding. I give you the credit in all I do and know you are directing my paths.

My part is to believe it and say it—
God's part is to manifest His promises.

Ask God to reveal a scripture describing your true identity and then pray it as a believing prayer:

Step 3: PURPOSE

FIND THE PURPOSE IN THE PAIN

Lori's Story

There's more to my story. I experienced a personal 9/11 many years prior to my son's incarceration.

At 17 years old, I was raped by a trusted boyfriend. The dream to save myself for my future husband on our wedding day was stolen from me.

Out of pain I kept that secret for 23 years.

Out of pain I used alcohol and drugs to numb the hate. Out of the pain I believed the lie that suicide was the answer.

Hopelessness carried me to the top of the college football stadium where I fearlessly sat on the railing. I knew to end it all I simply needed to let go. I wanted to let go. I did let go.

At that very moment something grabbed me. I hesitated. In that hesitation, the Jesus I heard stories about as a little girl became very real to me. I knew he was there to save me. He was my first responder—my rescuer. I believed. He became my Living Hope.

The purpose in my pain was to find Jesus. I began reading his word, attending a bible believing church, and connected with praying women from Stonecroft. Today, I'm a voice of hope and co-direct Christian Communicators equipping other women to share their stories.

STEP 4: ENJOY

ENJOY A CHANGED LIFE!

Hope gives you a new perspective and joy improves your health.

A cheerful heart is good medicine,
But a crushed spirit dries up the bones.
Proverbs 17:22 NIV

Take a JOY BREAK today and watch your health improve!
- Celebrate something little in a big way—be creative!
- Exercise compassion—be skilled at giving.
- Embrace someone—at least for 30 seconds.
- Break the sound barrier—with your laugh!
- Bust out a dance move—in public!

This will make you smile...

"Ask, using my name, and you will receive, and you will have abundant joy." - John 16:24 NLT

Be the spark that ignites your friend's laughter. - Bonnie Jensen

We don't laugh because we're happy—we're happy because we laugh. - William James

That day is lost in which one has not laughed. - French Proverb

Life is a mirror – we see the best results when we smile.

J esus   **O** thers   **Y** ou

THINK H.O.P.E. EVERY DAY

Chapter 3 - Heartwork
Use the tools from this chapter and start digging for HOPE

Step 1) HEAL: The honest pain in my heart is:

The false protectors I use are:

Step 2) OVERCOME: My true identity is:

Taking my thoughts captive reveals I believe this lie:

This is today's believing prayer from God's Word:
Thank you, Lord,

Step 3) PURPOSE: The purpose in my pain is to:

Step 4) ENJOY: Today's joy break is:

~ 4 ~

FEAR vs. HOPE

*Fear was designed by God to give our bodies the sudden
bursts of strength and speed we need in emergencies.
But when fear becomes a permanent condition, it can paralyze
the spirit, keeping us from taking the risks of generosity,
love and vulnerability that characterize citizens of
God's Kingdom.*
-David Neff, *Christians Who Fear Too Much*, Christianity Today

Step 1 : HEAL your hurting heart by choosing hope.
Have you been invited to go on a mission trip or share your story with a large group? You trust God and know he is calling you to step out of your comfort zone to speak but you reply with a fearful *no.*

Has God convicted you of reaching out to a troubled relative or friend but you are afraid of not having the right words?

Fear always costs you something. It costs relationships, time, money, dreams and even health. That kind of fear is not from God but a force of darkness. Author Stormie Omartian writes in *Lord, I Want To Be Whole* that the only fear you are to have is the fear of God, a respect for God's authority and power.

Hope, however, makes things happen! Hope restores, renews and rebuilds broken lives. Sometimes hope is hard to wrap our hearts around and I found these simple definitions to be helpful.

FEAR: Expecting something BAD to happen.

HOPE: Expecting something GOOD to happen.

How would you answer this question—Can you have both fear and hope at the same time? Yes or No

The answer is yes, but no. As a believer, we have Living Hope but as humans, fear resides in our wounded hearts.

Once the fear is exposed and processed, the hope buried inside comes alive again.

PERSONAL INVENTORY – take your first thought captive and write *Bad* or *Good*.

I expect something (BAD OR GOOD) to happen in my:

Marriage: _____   Children: _____

Finances: _____   Relationships: _____

Dreams: _____   Future: _____

Sin: _____   Death: _____

FEAR PARALYZES HOPE PROPELS
FEAR SUFFOCATES HOPE SOARS
FEAR SQUELCHES HOPE SHOUTS
FEAR HURTS HOPE HEALS

The Physical Side of Fear
(from *More Excellent Health* by Henry Wright)

Anxiety
Multiple Sclerosis
Eczema
Acne
Diabetes Mellitus
Overeating
Insomnia
Fibromyalgia
AND MORE....

High Blood Pressure
Gastrointestinal System
Chronic Inflammation
Hives/Shingles
Fatigue
Depression
Sinus Infections
Panic Attacks

Wright believes fear is the number one plague in the world.

What physical symptoms from fear are you experiencing?

The Spiritual Side of Fear

Robs our dreams
Stifles our giving
Paralyzes our faith
Weakens our spiritual muscles

Steals our joy
Act like unbelievers
Locks our hearts
Destroys our body, soul, spirit

What spiritual symptoms from fear are you experiencing?

Fear must not be a way of life!

What are you expecting BAD to happen?

How is it infecting your life today?

How is it infecting your future?

Step 2: OVERCOME - Fear with HOPE!

As an overcomer, you already have all the hope you need to heal your hurting heart and live emotionally pain-free.

Remember, Jesus—The Living Hope is in you. It's a matter of taking your thoughts captive and speaking truth over the lies. Choosing hope over fear.

These words are promises and God does not set us up to fail. As overcomers, we have the mind of Christ to think HOPE!

For God has not given us a spirit of fear but of power and of love and of sound mind. 2 Timothy 1:7 NKJV

For who has known the mind of the Lord that he may instruct them? But we have the mind of Christ. I Corinthians 2:16 NIV

Therefore, are you operating with the mind of Christ or is fear controlling your thoughts?

On the scale below, where do you see yourself?

Total FEAR--Total HOPE

The fears of the wicked will be fulfilled;
the hopes of the godly will be granted.
Proverbs 10:24

When believers are living in fear, they do things that re-resemble the wicked and their fears are fulfilled.

Fear of forgiving brings conditional love resulting in broken relationships which is what they ultimately feared.

Fear of failure brings selfishness resulting in dead dreams which is what they ultimately feared.

The fears of 'acting like' the wicked will be fulfilled.

But the HOPES of the godly (overcomer, the one acting rightly)—will be granted!

Use THE HOPE PRAYER on page 40 to help you identify fear and choose hope.

(Remember to identify which part of you is fearful).

THE HOPE PRAYER

Lord, the_____part of me acknowledges
my fear of_____(see below) allowing me to act like
the wicked one and overtake me.

My fear of_____(identify fear)
in (circumstance) has caused me to experience
(identify all emotional and physical pain).

I have the mind of Christ and choose hope expecting
something good even in the bad.

Thank you for granting my desire to live in hope. In
the Name of Jesus Christ of Nazareth. Amen.

Possible Fears you may face:

Fear of the future	Fear of disaster	Fear of hoping
Fear of forgiving	Fear of dreaming	Fear of death
Fear of the future	Fear of weakness	Fear of rejection
Fear of a huge task	Fear of loss	Fear of change

Emotional or Physical Pain caused by FEAR:

Anxiousness	Discouragement	Depression
Stress	Joylessness	Condemnation
Bitterness	Pressure	Embarrassment
Inadequacy	Loneliness	Guilt
Sleeplessness	Disappointment	Apathy
Pride	Frustration	Suicidal thoughts
Insecurity	Anger	Selfishness
Worthlessness	Headaches	Defensiveness

Does any other fear or pain come to mind?

Step 3: PURPOSE in the pain – God never wastes anything—not even our fears.

Best-selling author Stormie Omartian is a survivor of child abuse.

"My definition of emotional health," Omartian writes, "is having total peace about who you are, what you're doing and where you're going, both individually and in relationship to those around you."

Her book, *Lord, I Want to Be Whole,* is a great resource to help you release the past, live in obedience to God, recognize and resist the real enemy and stand strong when facing difficulties.

Stormie writes about finding Treasures in the Darkness--

God is God when things are bad as well as when they are good, when it is dark as well as when it is light.

Sometimes the darkness around us is not darkness of death but rather a darkness like in a womb, where we are growing and being made ready for birth. Just as a child in the womb knows nothing of the world waiting for him, so we do not realize the greatness of God's purpose for us.

The Bible says, "I will give you treasures of darkness." (Isaiah 45:3).

Certain valuable experiences in the Lord can only be found in the dark times.

Can you see how God used a dark time in your life to grow you in some way?

How can it become a treasure in the darkness?

Step 4: ENJOY a changed life – Choose HOPE!

Which JOY BREAK will you take today or this week?

- Write all your fears on a helium-filled balloon and release it. The balloon is filled with HOPE and carries all your fears to God who sees and receives your step of faith.

- Write your fears on a piece of paper and safely burn it.

- Memorize this believing prayer: *Thank you, Lord, that I do not have the spirit of fear but I have power, love and sound mind over every situation.* (from 2 Timothy 1:7)

THINK H.O.P.E. EVERY DAY

Chapter 4 - Heartwork

Use the tools from this chapter and start digging for HOPE

Step 1 - HEAL: The biggest fear I am facing today is...

Which part of me is in fear?

This fear could be infecting me physically in this way:

Step 2 - OVERCOME: Taking my thoughts captive reveals I'm believing this lie:

Today, I pray the Hope Prayer and release all fear trusting God alone to be my Protector and Hope.

Step 3 - PURPOSE: God, show me how can I find purpose in my pain through the darkness of the womb?

Step 4 - ENJOY: Today my Joy Break is_____

~ 5 ~

THE KEY TO FORGIVENESS

STEP 1: HEAL your hurting heart through forgiveness.

Assuming you are getting honest with your emotional pain, it is likely unforgiveness is surfacing to the top.

People hurt us by things they do—or don't do.
People hurt us by things they say—or don't say.
People hurt us intentionally—or unintentionally.

Hurting people hurt people!

Forgiveness breaks that hurting cycle. Through Jesus' selfless sacrifice and his forgiveness at the cross, he brought hope to all humanity. Because you have that Living Hope, you too— can forgive and be a voice of hope.

When you choose not to forgive, you are seeking justice. Is it your job to administer justice?

No. It's God's job to administer justice.

He will judge the world in justice;
And rule the nations with fairness.
Psalm 9:8 NLT

When you choose to forgive, everybody wins—you win and are set free; the offender is in God's hands with the opportunity to receive grace and mercy; and God wins— He is glorified. Don't ever be sorry for doing the right thing!

Do you REALLY know what forgiveness is?
Do you REALLY know what forgiveness is not?

In the midst of emotional pain, truth and lies are mixed up in our brain. Our thinking becomes distorted. It's important to untwist the lies and focus on the truth about forgiveness.

The chart on page 46 may help you do the UN-twist about forgiveness.

Forgiveness IS		Forgiveness is NOT
A Choice – Satan loses his power and healing begins.	2 Cor.2:10,11	A Feeling – if you wait until you feel like for- giving, it won't happen
Letting the offender off YOUR hook.	Romans 12:19	Letting them off God's hook. Trust God!
Remembering the pain – it is possible to remember and not re-live the pain.	Psalm 147:3	Hanging on to the pain and remaining a victim.
For your sake -be free! will respond.	Luke 6:37-38	A guarantee the offender
Obedience	Mark 11:25	An Option
Freedom to love – you take more risks to love and be loved.	Galatians 5:13	Freedom to sin – since God forgives I can do what I want.
Strength	Phil. 4:13	Weakness
Costly & Rewarding – Jesus died, but gained everything.	Luke 23:34	Easy – dying to self is not easy but possible.
Love – the best way to get rid of an enemy is to make him your friend!	2 Cor. 2:7-8	Love without action- do something kind to the offender.

Do you know the difference between Forgiveness and Sorry?
Forgiveness is towards sin. Sorry is towards accidents.

Step 2: OVERCOME by using the key to forgiveness.

The key to forgiveness is not only forgiving the offender for WHAT he/she did, but forgiving HOW it made you feel.

A physical wound never heals when infected. An emotionally wounded heart never heals when infected with emotional pain. You heal the pain—you heal your heart. No more band-aides reminding you of a festering wound! A healed heart may leave a scar, but scars aren't painful.

**Remember the pain to help others,
but don't re-live the pain through an unhealed heart.**

For years, I forgave that trusted friend for raping me, but I often re-lived that night of betrayal. Did I REALLY forgive him? Did I really WANT to forgive him? Do I not have enough faith to forgive? That tug of war went on for 23 years.

Wayne and Jeannine Allen of Freedom Ministries gave me the key that unlocked my heart. When I forgave him for raping me AND HOW HE MADE ME FEEL (dirty, rejected, betrayed, not listened to, guilty, ashamed, hateful, not loved, not valued, confused, divided—do you get the idea), I healed.

I remember that moment so I can share my story with other women who have been wounded—but I don't re-live the pain and stay stuck in the mire like I did for 23 long years.

How many years have you been trying to forgive and forget? How's it working for you? Use the key.

What offense do you need to remember but not relive?

Forgiveness and Blessing Prayer

Lord, the _____part of me comes to you and I choose to forgive rather than seek justice.

I forgive _____(name) for _____(offense) causing me to feel _____(emotional pain). I take back any ground (joy, peace, love, etc.) stolen by the enemy through my unforgiveness. Bless _____(name) with your love. In Jesus' name. Amen

EMOTIONAL PAIN WORDS

Abandoned	Accused	Alone	Always wrong
Anxious	Ashamed	Belittled	Bitter
Betrayed	Condemned	Confused	Controlled
Cut off	Deceived	Defenseless	Defeated
Destroyed	Dirty	Discouraged	Disappointed
Embarrassed	Exhausted	Empty	Failure
Fearful	Frustrated	Hopeless	Hate
Hurt	Humiliated	Ignored	Inadequate
Insecure	Insignificant	Judged	Lonely
Lied to	Lost	Manipulated	Misunderstood Not
cared for	Not valued	No good	Not cherished Not
listened to	Overwhelmed	Paralyzed	Pressure
Rejected	Resentful	Revenge	Ruined
Sad	Scared	Stepped on	Trapped
Tricked	Ugly	Unaccepted	Unfairly judged
Unloved	Vulnerable	Weak	Worthless

What other emotional pain words come to your mind?

Ask God to reveal who you need to forgive. Don't forget to include yourself or even God?

You may want to create a timeline of your life which can reveal specific events or ages where you experienced emotional pain.

Step 3: PURPOSE in your pain – Forgiveness sets you free!

RENEE'S STORY

A drunk driver killed Renee Napier's 20-year-old daughter, Meagan, and her friend Lisa May 11, 2002. The 24-year-old driver, Eric Smallridge, received a 22-year sentence.

Shortly after Meagan's death, Renee turned a negative into a positive by giving DUI presentations to high schools, colleges, and a multitude of audiences. However, she knew something was missing.

Renee needed to forgive the young man who accidentally took her daughter's life. She went to Eric at the Florida Penitentiary giving him an incredible gift— forgiveness. He struggled to receive it. He couldn't even forgive himself. When he did, he found freedom behind bars.

In April 2010, Eric, as an inmate bound by shackles, joined Renee to share their story. She went on to plea for Eric's early release. In November 2012, he was released from prison eleven years early. Today he tours with Renee offering a powerful message of forgiveness and hope.

Grammy nominated singer Matthew West was inspired by her story. West wrote and recorded the top- of-the-charts hit *Forgiveness* released on his 2012 *Into The Light* album. The songwriter puts it this way:

It'll clear the bitterness away. It can even set a prisoner free. There is no end to what its power can do… The prisoner that it really frees is you.

When I met Renee at a Matthew West event, she said, "I lost a daughter, but I gained a son."

That is forgiveness.

STEP 4:   ENJOY a changed and healthy life by starting a Kindness Revolution.

Barry K. Weinhold, University of Colorado, lists physiological and psychological benefits resulting from being kind rather than bitter:

Strong immune system	Reduces physical pain
Increases body warmth	Develops sense of joy
Improves weight control	Promotes optimism
Drops blood pressure	Provides more energy
Enhances relaxation	Reduces stomach acid
Slows down cancer	Decreases loneliness
Relieves lupus symptoms	Decreases depression
Relieves asthma symptoms	Increases longevity

Get obsessed....with kindness!

At a drive through, pay the tab of the person behind you.
Each day for 30 days do something kind for someone.
Pick up trash.
Adopt a soldier.
Send flowers—just because.
Have a charity day at work.
Give hugs to the hard-to-hug.

What is your idea?

How has it improved your health?

THINK H.O.P.E. EVERY DAY

Chapter 5 - Heartwork
Use tools from this chapter to start digging for HOPE

STEP 1: HEAL: The person I need to forgive today is....

Which part of me needs to forgive?

The offense and pain that person caused me is...

STEP 2: OVERCOME: Taking my thoughts captive reveals that I have believed the lie that

Today, I pray the Forgiveness Prayer and release all offenses and pain trusting God alone to be my Protector and Hope.

STEP 3: PURPOSE: God, how can I find purpose in my pain by blessing those whom I've forgiven?

STEP 4: ENJOY: Today, my Joy Break is_____

~ 6 ~

Hope deferred (unrelenting disappointment) makes
your heart sick but a longing fulfilled is the tree of life.
Proverbs 13:12 NIV

THE ROOT OF DEPRESSION

In my experience, depression is unmet expectations rooted in selfish longings.

However, God placed the longings of significance, success, security, spirituality and intimacy in us to be filled by Him alone. It's *from* him and *for* him those longings flow.

Without this understanding, we seek to fulfill longings through artificial means—people, places and things. This creates unhealthy expectations resulting in disappointment, disappointment and more disappointment.

Godly roots produce godly fruits

When our longings are rooted in God, our expectations flow through Jesus to grow godly fruits like those listed in Galatians 5:22—joy, peace, patience, kindness, goodness, faithfulness, gentleness and self-control.

Often times, however, our God-given longings are rooted in self-serving soil which produces shallow expectations and rotten fruit.

Some of these fruits are impurity, idolatry, hatred, discord, jealousy, fits of rage, selfish ambition. More are listed in Galatians 5:19.

When our lives are led by misplaced longings producing unmet expectations bearing rotten fruit—our hearts get sick. Depression sets in which leads to other health related problems. Life looks hopeless.

Have you put your longing for **significance** in a spouse (misplaced longing) only to have them ask for a divorce (unmet expectation), leaving you bitter and betrayed (bad fruit)?

Have you put your longing for **success** in your job (misplaced longing) expecting a promotion but received a termination notice due to downsizing (unmet expectation), leaving you angry and depressed (bad fruit)?

Have you put your longing for **security** in a 401K (misplaced longing) but lost most of it due to the poor economy (unmet expectation), leaving you feeling like a failure (bad fruit)?

Have you put your longing for **spirituality** in a pastor (misplaced longing) who had an affair and left his church (unmet expectation), leaving you confused and disappointed (bad fruit)?

Have you put longing for **intimacy** in the hands of a trusted friend (misplaced longing) and they betrayed you (unmet expectation), leaving you bitter (bad fruit)?

It's important to note that expectations follow the longings. Putting expectations in people or possessions will disappoint us.

Putting expectations in Jesus and what he wants to accomplish, never disappoints us. Often, it's more than we imagine.

Look at the Life of Jesus

Significance: Religious leaders expected to crucify Jesus and got their wish—but Jesus rose from the dead. (John 19 & 20)

Success: The disciples expected a typical day of fishing with Jesus—but Jesus gave them a Savior. (Luke 5:1-11).

Security: The crowds expected a political leader to set up a new kingdom against Rome—but Jesus provided an eternal kingdom to overthrow sin. (John 3:16)

Spirituality: The religious leaders expected miracles—but Jesus gave them the Creator of miracles. (Matthew 12:38-45)

Intimacy: A woman expected to be healed just by touching Jesus' cloak—but Jesus stopped and called her daughter telling her to go in peace and be freed from suffering. (John 5:21- 34)

**GODLY LONGINGS + GODLY EXPECTATIONS=
GODLY FRUIT**

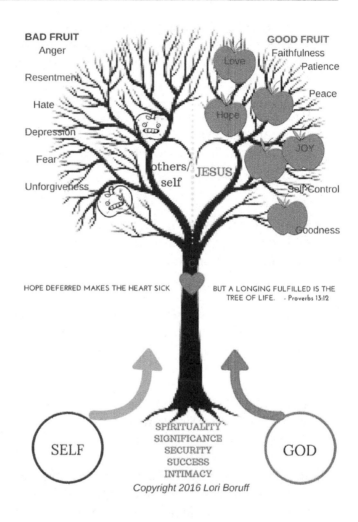

BAD FRUIT
Anger
Resentment
Hate
Depression
Fear
Unforgiveness

GOOD FRUIT
Faithfulness
Patience
Peace

Love

Hope

JOY

Self-Control

Goodness

others/ JESUS
self

HOPE DEFERRED MAKES THE HEART SICK

BUT A LONGING FULFILLED IS THE
TREE OF LIFE.   - Proverbs 13:12

SPIRITUALITY
SIGNIFICANCE
SECURITY
SUCCESS
INTIMACY

SELF

GOD

Copyright 2016 Lori Boruff

I am the vine, you are the branches.
If any man remains in me, and I in him,
he will bear much fruit; apart from me, you can do
nothing.
John 15:5 NIV

SIGNIFIGANCE: We want to matter. Is your importance rooted in selfishness? Are you putting your expectations in people, careers or circumstances? What fruit does that produce?

SUCCESS: We long to achieve more. Is it for your own personal satisfaction? Are you expectations in your spouse, children, boss, financial account? What fruit does that produce?

SECURITY: We love to feel safe and secure. Are my expectations in my position, possessions or people? What fruit does that produce?

SPIRITUALITY: We desire spiritual experiences. Are my expectations in religion, a pastor, or events? Does that fruit last or does it spoil?

INTIMACY: We long to belong. We long to connect. Who or what do you depend on to fulfill that longing? What fruit does that produce?

Use the diagram on page 55 and look again at these longings. Focus on the right side of the tree. Start at the root (God); put your expectations in what Jesus wants to do in your life, and see the lasting fruit it produces.

STEP 2: OVERCOME misplaced longings with believing prayers!

SIGNIFICANCE: Pray the bold print!

Is this a joyous choir I hear? No, it is the Lord himself exulting over you in happy song. Zeph. 3:18 TLB

Lord, is that a joyous choir I hear? No, it's you exulting over me with a happy song. Thank you!

SECURITY:

...the one the LORD loves rests between His shoulders. Deuteronomy 33:12 NIV

Thank you, Lord that you love me and I can rest between your shoulders.

SUCCESS:

He shall succeed, because God is able to make him to succeed. Romans 14:4 TEV

Thank you, Lord that I will succeed because you are able to make me succeed!

SPIRITUALITY:

Now if we be dead with Christ, we believe that we shall also live with him. Romans 6:8 KJV

Thank you, Jesus that I live forever with you!

INTIMACY:

Now all praise to God for his wonderful kindness to us and his favor that he has poured out upon us because we belong to his dearly loved Son. Ephesians 1:6 TLB

Thank you, God, for your wonderful kindness and favor because I belong to your dearly loved Son.

Read Psalm 33 and find all five longings!

STEP 3: PURPOSE in your pain – Write your story!

Heal: What difficulties have you faced? What pain have you experienced from that difficulty?

Overcome: How have you overcome the lies you believed with truth? How has your true identity empowered you to live like an overcomer?

Purpose: What purpose have you found in your pain? How can God use it to help others?

Enjoy: How are you enjoying your changed life?

Step 4: ENJOY a changed life—Where will your hope take you?

Since you have found HOPE in the ruins, I trust you've also discovered a fresh vision and new dreams for the future. Define those dreams and keep moving forward!

My vision for the future is:

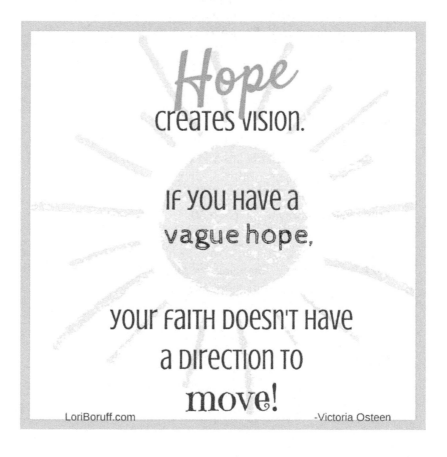

Hope creates vision. If you have a vague hope, your faith doesn't have a direction to move!

LoriBoruff.com   -Victoria Osteen

THINK H.O.P.E. EVERY DAY

Chapter 6 - Heartwork
Use tools from this chapter to start digging for HOPE

STEP 1: HEAL: I confess my longings have been rooted in selfishness, my expectations have been misplaced and it produces rotten fruit. Be specific.

STEP 2: OVERCOME: I receive the truth that my longings are God-given. I choose to put my expectations in what Jesus wants to do in my life and I'm grateful for the good fruit it produces.

Pray believing prayers on page 50.

STEP 3: PURPOSE: Changing my perspective changes my story. How has my story changed?

STEP 4: ENJOY: Today, my Joy Break is_____

~ 7 ~

HOPE IN THE RUINS

May the God of hope fill you with all joy and peace as you trust in him, so that you may overflow with hope by the power of the Holy Spirit.   Romans 15:13 NIV

Full of hope; you'll relax, confident again; you'll look around, sit back, and take it easy.   Job 11:18 MSG

This is hope we have as an anchor of the soul, a hope both sure and steadfast.   Hebrews 6:19 NASB

Now faith is the substance of things hoped for, the evidence of things not seen.   Hebrews 11:1 KJV

I wait quietly before God, for my hope is in him.
Psalm 62:5 NLT

Find rest, O my soul, in God alone; my hope comes from him.
Psalm 62:5 NIV

I will always have hope...
Psalm 71:14

~ 8 ~

H.O.P.E. RESOURCES

Suggested authors:

Rusty Boruff   incarceration, addiction, restoration,
Carol Kent   incarceration, fear, longings, forgiveness
Cecil Murphey   abuse, caregivers, overcoming, fears
Charles Swindoll   parenting, hope and healing

Stormie Omartian   healing, hope, purpose, forgiveness Liz
Curtis Higgs   healing, hope, purpose, humor

Twila Belk   healing, humor, hope, inspiration

Lynn Eib   hope, illness, cancer

Online Ministries:

LoriBoruff.com   coaching, speaking, hope, healing
OneEighty.org   incarceration, addiction, restoration
Speakupforhope.org   incarceration, families
Stonecroft.org   serving, prayer, bible studies
Freedomministriesqc.com   counselling, hope, healing
Griefshare.org   grief, hope, healing

Speaker Training:

ChristianCommunicators.com   training, message, business

ABOUT THE AUTHOR

LORI BORUFF

Since Lori found hope and freedom from the emotional pain of rape and raising two boys on difficult paths, she isn't afraid of taking risks. She shares her story with hurting women.

Lori is a favorite keynote speaker leaving audiences connected, comforted and changed. Her messages are honest, heartfelt and sprinkled with humor to lighten heavy hearts.

She serves as Christian Communicators Co-director educating, validating and launching speakers to the next level of their ministry. She is a trusted life-coach for women who are ready to lose their worry and live their wonderful.

"Within two weeks of using the tools Lori shared with me, I made important breakthroughs in areas I was stuck."- TK

Lori loves the lighter side of life spending time at the lake with her husband, Rick. They enjoy their two sons, one beautiful daughter-in-law and two fast-growing grandsons. They reside in Illinois.

Email: lori@loriboruff.com   **Website:** LoriBoruff.com
Find her on FB and Instagram!

THINK H.O.P.E. EVERY DAY

Heartwork
Reproducible worksheet

Step 1) HEAL: The honest pain in my heart is:

Step 2) OVERCOME: My true identity is:

Taking my thoughts captive reveals I believe this lie:

This is today's believing prayer from God's Word:
Thank you, Lord,

Step 3) PURPOSE: The purpose in my pain is to:

Step 4) ENJOY: Today's joy break is: